From Stressed To Blessed

A crucial cure through poetry

Joey Tyson

BookLeaf Publishing

India | USA | UK

Made with ❤ on the BookLeaf Publishing Platform
www.bookleafpub.in
www.bookleafpub.com

Dedication

This book is dedicated to anyone who knows what it feels like to be the source of all the chaos in their own life.

Preface

While on my path to healing. I wrote poetry. I feel every word of these poems very deeply. Please enjoy, but do not take them lightly.

Acknowledgements

To everyone who hurt me; without you these wouldn't be possible.
Thank you for the lessons, it has been a blessing.

1. My Love For You

My love for you was always known.
But just like me it had to grow.
Not only has it molded me.
It turned me into someone I didn't want to be.
For that love of yours was surely fake,
How much can one kid take.
In my heart I always knew,
I'd forever be confused.
My love for you was never lost.
But it surely had a cost.
Was more pricey than a dollar.
Why did you only holler.
Nothing done but another fight.
Oh, this burden it isn't light.
When will someone finally say,
I'm here for you and then stay.
My love for you has new direction,
Simply with less affection.
Who would you even bother,
Trying to protect your daughter.

2. Adored You

When I said I adored you
I saw a smile on your face
One that turns blue skies to gray

When I said I adored you
Your ego came out to play
Filled with words to hurt me
Then just run away

When I said I adored you
I meant in every way
Not only when its sunny
But as you walked away

3. Love With No Conditions

All these words mean the same thing, even when said
differently.
I always felt no matter what, you wouldn't want to be
with me.
Sober or not, I wasn't going to be someone you'd see
equally.
Imagine that the day I give it up entirely, you've already
cut me out and erased me.
Little do you know, I'm the one who plants the seeds,
waters them and waits patiently.
Helping people to grow into better versions x3.
You know they say be the person you think you'd need.
So I started loving unconditionally.

4. Power Of Mind

The mind is a powerful thing,
So why is mine always reminding me of who I was
before those things you did to me.
How can my brain not care about giving that space
away,
Allowing such shit to occupy its time.
When will it realize that fueling itself with all these lies,
Only keeps me stagnant on the inside.

5. Bad For You

What do you do when you miss someone who is bad for you?
You turn off your phone and do not curl up in bed.
Then tell yourself, all the things they didn't.
Like how much you are loved, damn you are so pretty or something close to those above.
Communicate to yourself like no one else does.
You speak your language of love.
Look in the mirror and do nothing but smile.
You deserve to see it once in a while.
You may even learn why smiles can brighten room.
As you smile at you.
For you.
About you.
Know you can do this for them too.
Who?
Oh, you forgot about the one you said you missed.
Now don't forget you were smiles just a second ago.
And I know you have the power to control your ego.
So,
Step back.
Smile again.
You are so divine.
Your aura shines.

Sometimes people only glow when left alone.
So, take the lessons and know how to grow.
Shit happens, you've loved and will be loved again.
Don't let a mindset be your downfall from heaven.
Get up, smile again.
One for you and two for them.
Now be a peace with what you just did.
I'm proud of you for accepting it for what it is.
Now once more, yes you guessed it.
Smile like you never have before.
With an inner peace only you can adore.

6. Get What You Give

Why do I feel so torn between loving and leaving,
One day it's great and we get along.
But the next day its far from anything I want.
What hurts Is knowing I gave you every tool needed to
use me.
I let you in and let you know what was needed to love
me.
Even worse, I told you what to look for to know that I
was in fact in love with you.
But I don't understand why someone would use their
own love against them.
To know how someone loves is a blessing of its own.
You should not use it to fuel an ego.
Or fix parts of you that are not whole.
To get what you give you have to look in the mirror once
in a while.
Show yourself what it really is you are giving.
Half ass love or just a bad attitude?
Know your role in the things or people around you.

7. Talk About Everything

We used to talk about everything,
From a place of understanding.
It was so exciting for me to be with someone who just
knew me.
I still had my doubts,
I should've just let my guard down without a second
thought.
If I did maybe we would still have things to talk about.
Or maybe that's what I do wrong.
Start to blame myself for not being vulnerable all along.
That may just be what they want.
Get a look into my mind to see where my heads at
To learn all my dos and don'ts, to then feed off my soul
Because we used to talk about everything
But as of lately I just feel like they have a piece of me
And maybe that's why they don't feel the need to say
anything.

8. Stunted

Simply a lost kid from a broken home,
Trying to soothe my soul.
What started as my parent's drama.
Slowly turned into my trauma.
Little did they know,
How much I didn't grow.
Stunted by my father's ego.
Till the day I was sent away.
What hurt me then,
Helps me fly today.
All I ever wanted was for him to be proud,
He made it clear I let him down.
Not knowing where I'd go,
I had to figure things out on my own.
I found a place and made it home.
Learned some things and had to grow.
Coming from a broken home,
Left my soul with plenty holes.
The amount of love I didn't get,
Kept me from being a kid.

9. ♫ ♪ ♫ ♫ ♪ ♩.

When I hear a song, I can't help but think how every
note is its own beat.
You know, separately they have their own groove.
Under certain circumstance they can sound out of tune.
This is kind of how I see me and you.
While I hear my notes come out softly with little vibrato,
I also hear yours sound heavy and short with staccato.
Now I know you have perfected your note, belting it out
through all circumstance.
You even learned to dance.
But what if you could be more than that?
More than just a note played beautifully.
What if we could match our grooves?
I play beautifully and you play beautifully right after too.
Complementing each other's tones.
Filling in those gaps so the other can breathe.
Before we know it, we played a symphony.
Composed by us both, effortlessly.
I like to think it is that easy
Us, writing symphonies or ballads or even a song two
notes long.
With you, id write just about anything.
Knowing that love is like music and sometimes we forget
to sing.

10. Your Love

I'd be lying if I said I never felt your love.

The type of love I didn't think existed.

Pouring out of you, filling pieces of me until I felt complete.

I've spent so much time living but not feeling whole underneath.

I never believed in soul mates or twin flames,

Until that first time you saw me.

I saw a fire ignite your soul.

Our eyes met consistently.

Telling each other everything, silently.

We had a whole conversation in front of everybody, nonverbally.

I surely had no questions that it was meant to be.

You were a blessing; I thanked God for you daily.

I never thought it would end so soon.

But that's my favorite part about us too.

We were never meant to be forever (although I may have liked that.)

I was there when you were losing your mother.

Watched you cry, held your hand.

Was nothing but solid.

Then you let me in.

To break down, not defend.

Which parts of you were broken.
I fell hard.
Fast off my path to enlightenment, I entertained it.
Knowing it would hurt, I did it anyways.
Loved you unconditionally, while you picked me apart to
fit your needs.
You took to my hobbies.
I noticed our similarities.
You were such a blessing.
I pray you live life more authentically.
But what I am most thankful for is what you gave me,
A lesson in what it's like to try to love me.

11. The Fog

Some may say the storm will pass.
Skies can't always be gray.
To them I say
What if it's more than gray skies that make me worry.
What about the fog in the morning?
Even though it sits in the sunrise in all its glory
You just never know what it may be holding.

12. Grace

For the grace of God is all you need.
Be always thankful, never greedy.

13. Words

A few words could've changed everything.

But as I looked at you, I couldn't even say one thing.

I so desperately wanted you to hear me.

I felt that you thought you knew me.

I can't be only how you view me.

I am so much more.

If you only focus on where I went wrong or point out all my flaws.

Then that's how you'll perceive me.

The bad guy,

I wish people spent more time looking at the good in others.

To stop limiting what others can be.

To stop limiting how others are seen.

14. Stupid

How stupid can I really be,
If just about everyone I meet learns something from me.
I enjoy planting seeds that can grow into something
mind altering.
Hopefully leading to changes throughout the whole
being.

How stupid can I really be,
To not notice what others can teach me.
It's not often people will change the way they think.
How could you not want to always be growing.

How stupid can I really be,
Missing opportunities to acknowledge the people around
me.
Unable to see the divinity beneath.
Losing all faith in humanity.

15. Adore Me

I refuse to give you, my energy.
Always calls when he just wants to use me.
Something i learned recently, timing is everything.
So pay attention every time the phone rings and take
good inventory of what they may be lacking.
Do they call knowing you'll fill that hole.
I assume so.
Not anymore.
I no longer wish to be that piece he needs to fill his
energy.
I no longer wish to have you put me on hold when you
decide I'm not good enough.
But only for a week or so, then he realizes just how
much he feeds off my soul.
That sounds pretty brutal but if you know, you know.
I don't mind being people's sunshine.
But at the end of the day there's no way I can remain the
same while you continue to change.
I only pray that one day he will adore me just as much
when I walk away.

16. To Say

To say this was a waste,
Well, that'd be a lie.
To say I'd ever love the same,
I couldn't if I tried.
To say it's confusing,
That couldn't be more true.
To say that I love you,
Took longer for me than you.

To say I'm not as trusting,
Shouldn't be a surprise.
To say things haven't changed,
Makes me miss when we first locked eyes.
To say we've grown for the better,
That I can't deny.

To say moving on is easy,
I guess I never tried.
To say you're mine forever,
Would make me smile every time.
To say I could live without you,
I'd never want to try.

17. Sisterly Love

Sometimes I allow their lies to get me stuck in my mind.
Making me wonder that maybe I am the bad guy.
For my whole life it seems I've allowed her to make me
feel like I am a shitty human being.
I was always the problem.
I no longer wish to fit the script of the bullshit plot she
comes up with.
I know she has no interest in seeing things for my
perspective.
Or considering that I've grown and changed a bit.
It hurts, that she doesn't think I'm worth getting to
know.
I feel like while growing up I played my role.
Just to be shit on and abused.
I hold no hate nor put blame.
Just hope one day things can change.

18. Light

Focus on being the light,
For you can shine and help mankind.
Your beacon should guide and remind,
To stay on the positive side of mind.

19. The Path

What no one tells you about the road less traveled,
Is how it is a constant uphill battle paved with gravel.
Often leading far from what you know,
You can find any place and make it home.

20. Inspired

Am I inspired?
Absolutely.
With my faith in God
How could I not be.
Which you'd know,
Had you bothered to ask me.
I find the truth most appealing,
Often times, I just enjoy what resonates within me.

21. Simple Life

Life is a blessing.
Although that wasn't an easy lesson,
Try to find a better mindset to invest in.